THE WAY OF THE LOGOS

SEAN BYRNE

THE WAY OF THE LOGOS

THE ANCIENT ART OF MEDITATION

AGE-OLD BOOKS

Published by AGE-OLD BOOKS in N. Ireland

Copyright © Sean Byrne 2012

ISBN: 978-0-9540255-9-5

A catalogue record of this book is available from the British Library.

Contents

Introduction

Meditation is an art. And like every other art it takes time, dedication, and practise if it is to yield its best fruit.

Unlike other arts however, the fruit of meditation has a value that cannot be measured in gold. Its yield is even more precious than this. For it is a yield that outlasts the fads and fashions of temporal concerns, and brings us closer to the eternal verities, the God within: The Logos.

The fundamental fruit of meditation is a deepening and a strengthening of the life of the soul. Through it you are drawn nearer to the essence of all things. If you practise meditation, in time your understanding of both yourself and the world will change for the better. You will become enriched with a vital capacity to penetrate superficiality, wherever you find it. In meditation you are lighting an inner flame. Kindled initially in the heart and soul, this flame will, with patience and dedication, grow and slowly spread its light and warmth to all things you touch.

This flame is the spirit of wisdom, the wisdom of The Logos. Through it you acquire knowledge of your deeper self, that part of you which is normally encrusted over by the cares of the world and lies dormant always if it is not uncovered through this great art of stilling the mind.

Meditation creates an inner power of understanding. Through it you will learn to see the world more clearly, and understand it, and yourself, better. Truth and falsehood, joy and sorrow, the good and the bad in all things will become easily separated. You will learn how to discern, to choose, to live the good life, in the very best meaning of this term. And though you need never dispense with them entirely, there will be less and less need for external rules, rituals or laws to govern your life. For then your own inner God-given spirit will become your Guide in all the ups and downs of life.

In this way a sure knowledge of your purpose in life, a true sense of your own personal destiny, will emerge, and that most elusive and difficult of all goals - peace, happiness and contentment - will be yours.

The Silence

In a world where talk has never been cheaper

How much more precious and valuable

The virtue of Silence!

Take delight therefore in your silence.

Prize whatever portion of this rarity you are given.

Protect it like a pearl of great value.

Go to a secret place often

And bathe yourself there in the soothing rays

Of this jewel's tender light.

Seat yourself quietly and prayerfully

Away from the noisy world,

And there listen for the words that well up from the wisdom

That lives in the depths of your soul.

Who are you?

Come. Sit and listen.

Be embraced by the warmth of the wonderful silence

That is the essence of your soul's surging life.

Seek and drink from the Well of Knowledge.

If you do, you will learn of hidden wonders.

For out of your silence you will come to know

That you are much more than a mere name or number,

Or a crumbling body of clay.

Here, by the Well, a great truth will be revealed to you.

This is the truth of your own soul.

In every human being there lives a soul and a spirit.

It is our spirit, but it is also the Spirit of God.

Few there are however who know of this Being's great secrets.

For only those who come and sit by the blesséd Well of Silence

Can hear the one true Voice,

The Word of The Logos.

Listen!

The Well

The Master of all masters said:

'Come to me all you whose work is hard,

Whose load is heavy, and I will give you relief.'

Though coined in an age far distant

From the madrush of our own,

These words are newly minted

Each time you come to the Well

And drink of its Wisdom.

For the Angel spirit of Truth and Grace

Sits by this Well always,

Awaiting those whose hearts have been pierced,

Whose heads have been thorned

By the secret dart of the gods' love-magic.

These are the few like you who in every age and place

Find their way to this Well of Wisdom.

And here you are greeted always with a great joy.

Come and be seated therefore,

Just as the Lord once sat by the Well of Jacob and spoke

With the Woman of Samaria

Informing her of this same Great Spirit.

It says: You must let go of your past.

In your mediation you are gently urged to let go

Of the noise and the burden of your life,

Of its worries and its common cares.

Cast the eye of your thoughts

Upon the magic surface of this Well

And within its soft and silent undulations

Seek the face of your own soul.

If in Love you wait, this will appear.

You need only practise the virtues.

If you do not see, feel, or hear the true Voice straightaway

It is because the world

Has caked your soul over with its grime, its grit,

It rampant ugliness.

But though you may not yet see clearly

And though it may take time to polish,

The dulled beauty of your soul will eventually shine.

Be joyful!

For you have made your way to the Well of Life.

You may therefore count yourself among
the blessed.

And having now discovered it,

And it's beautiful Angel

You will surely come more often.

And as you come, you will slowly learn

To chip away the grime of your life

And the inner image of your true Self –

With all its magic and God-like wonder –

Will begin to show itself to you.

It is a wonderful thing to know your own soul!

For when you are once touched

By its truth and beauty,

You know that you have discovered

The way to the greatest of all truths.

To know your soul is to know the Way.

The Master of all masters said: I am the Way.

This is the Way of The Logos.

The Angel

Do not fear!

Do not fear the gaping wounds, the ugliness,

The soullessness that is the hallmark of
your time.

For a line has been cast to you,

And you have been hooked

With the secret, gentle voice of Love.

You can hear,

And now it draws you safely and securely

Into the Well,

The silence of your meditation.

Turn your thoughts often to your Angel

And try to feel or see this Being

In the warmth of your soul's imagination.

This Angel is your guide

And your Guardian always,

The sublimely free Spirit of Truth

Vibrantly alive at the centre of your soul

Pointing the Way to the fluttering meadows
of delight,

That mysterious place spoken of by the wise
ancients

Where the magic flower grows.

This is the mystic and eternal flower

Of pure spiritual Love.

Here only is the place where the ethereal
lotus grows and opens

Its flower-chalice to the sun.

For here only can its slender stem

Make its way up

From the dark depths of your past

Revealing the many-petalled blossom

Of your true Self.

This Self, buried amidst the debris

Of your life's wanderings

Reveals itself as the angelic voice of the Spirit.

It is the prophetic spirit of God

Crying amidst the machine-wrought
wilderness of the world.

Prepare yourself, it announces,

For a great new dawning,

A revelation which settles like a gentle dove

Upon the heads of all

Who truly long to know, love, and serve the
living God.

Turn away often therefore

From the madness of the world,

And sit by this Well of meditation.

Drink deep, for its waters spring

From an eternal fountain.

Immerse yourself in the silence

Of these soothing tones

Absorbing with devotion

Their healing, cleansing, and anointing power.

For only through devoted, constant, and prayerful meditation

Will you hear the voice of The Logos

Above the endless babble and chatter

Of the noisy world.

The Fish

Sitting by the soothing, healing Waters,

Remember always its grace, its depths,

Its fullness, and most of all its purity.

You will be healed!

It was here by the water's edge

That the wondrous Lord of Life

Said to the tired men endlessly toiling

For their crusts of bread:

'Come. Follow me. I will make you fishers of men.'

And effortlessly they rose and followed him.

For who can resist the golden charm

Of the unutterably sweet and gentle music

Which pours from the mouth of

The King of all Kings

And the Fish of all fishermen?

So come here often,

Sit silently and patiently

By this Well of Knowledge,

And do not doubt that you will eventually

Catch this Fish

And taste the wonder of its Wisdom.

The Child

Only when you withdraw from the teeming

Glittering round of you sense-bound life

And into the fragrant sweetness

Of your soul's ethereal truth

Will you know the meaning of peace.

And only when you have found this
otherworldly peace

Can you share it with your friend.

Never has the world more urgently needed

This gift of pure peace!

And it can come from no one else

But the universal Prince of peace, The Logos.

His Word echoes prophetically across the
oceans of time

And is heard, however faintly, in all the ages
of Man.

But only those who come and sit quietly

By the still water's edge,

And cup their hands, and drink

Of this holy water of meditation

Can hear this Voice clearly.

If you have ears to hear therefore, listen to
this Voice!

Awaken to the joyful Friend of your heart.

For he nestles there swaddled up

In the coils of your memory, and the memory
of the world,

Like a celestial flower-bud waiting to
burst forth

With its magic into your life,

Transforming it into a sweetly fragrant gift.

This offering, the flower of this spirit-child

Can grow in your soul.

But you need to feed it with the milk of
prayer,

Meditation, and devotion.

For know that you are this child's very
mother and father!

And in the gentle stirring of this bright new
Logos Being

Forming itself out of the ethereal essence
of your life

And the life of the world,

Know also that you are being guided in the
Way of Wisdom.

It is the self-same blessèd Way traversed by
the wise Magi of old

Who saw a star rise up out of the depths

Of their own hearts so powerfully, surely,
and brightly,

That it guided them to a secret place,

The place of this child's worldly and
miraculous birth.

Once born into the body of the Earth

This is the same spirit child that now and
forever

Longs to be reborn in the pure hearts

Of all those who openly profess

Their love of God.

This wise Child can become the very fruit of
your life

Once you consciously decide to nourish and
to cherish it.

For here is the true love-child.

Here is the white magic of all new life on Earth

Raised up out of the darkness of death.

Here is the spirit-birth within, yet beyond, the flesh,

Your initiation into the soul's truth.

This is the same truth the Master of all masters spoke

When he spoke of the astonishing truth of himself.

For the Way of The Logos is also the Way of initiation

Into the secret of the Divine Child.

Like you, this Child has a body of flesh and blood;

And like you also it has a soul.

But you will share in this secret of the Divine Child

Only when you come to know that his soul and yours

Can be united blissfully into One.

This Child is born and is grown out of the womb of Time

The womb that has also give birth to you,
to your soul,

And to these very words.

But whereas the body of earth withers and
dies,

The body of your soul has within it a new
seed.

This is the seed-Word

Of the immortal and living

Spirit of God: The Logos.

This Word never perishes, even if the stars

Fell from the sky.

Such is the eternal, the celestial

And the unutterably joyful

Wisdom of the Way.

The Way

The Way of Wisdom is the Way of watching

Of waiting and of praying.

Seated quietly and silently away from the
endless banter,

From the alluring, tinselled, and many-
coloured

Temptations of the noisy world,

Meditate upon these words

Wrought from the eternal Gospel of Love
and Peace.

They are the Way, and the very means

Of the great awakening!

Seek therefore the awakening

Of this Voice of Love in your heart,

Seek it like you have sought for nothing
ever before.

For, all other things of Earth

Fade in value like a morning mist

Once the wisdom of this Voice

Begins to sound and live in your heart.

For then you are awakening to the majestic
truth,

The reality of your very own soul.

In this awakening you are taking the cup of
your soul

And filling it with the Living Word

Of the Master of all masters,

And are offered up with him to the
supreme God.

Watch and wait with him in your heart
therefore, always.

For by watching and waiting with him

You are delivered of all the trials, terrible
or tiny,

That bedevil you and lure you into the falsity
of the world

And its ever-fading and withering
attractions.

And then, instead of this receding mirage

Of insatiable want and desire

You will see your true star rise above the
horizon of your life

And you will be led like a lamb

By the Voice of the true Shepherd into the
garden of delight

Where there is no more weeping,

No more anger, pain or loss.

This is the wonderful promise of all genuine

And surely guided mediation.

For it opens the doors of perception

To the hidden truths of the ethereal and eternal world.

Thus, in approaching this threshold of delight and joy

You become a witness to the Truth of the Spirit of God.

What choice have you therefore but to become its servant?

For who would not gladly serve this spirit of Truth

Once they have been touched

By its ineffable and ethereal charms?

In your meditation you seek the Way to this joy.

But lest you suffer from delusion

Remember always that this is not the Way of the world.

For, compared with the true Way of God

The way of the world is but a sprawling
monster's web of lies

Lurking outside the Garden of delight

Yet ever tightening its grip upon it.

The world seeks constantly to devour

This pure ethereal thing,

The delicate childlike flower of the
human soul.

What else can you do therefore but pray

For its release from the hating world?

For this claw which draws ever closer to you

As long as you sleep to its reality

Is but the false embrace of the world

And its bitter-sweet seductions –

The Judas Kiss of Death.

Remember these words therefore

That well up from the depths of the world

And bring to your meditation and your
prayer

The waking, watchful spirit of the Gospel of Love

Which longs to live ever more vibrantly and abundantly

In the hearts of all true lovers of The Logos and his precious Way.

The Cup

Take the Cup of your life and fill it here

At the Well of meditation.

For, if you do not learn to withdraw

From the terrible noise of your world,

It will wear you down to the very marrow of your bones

And make of you little more than one

Of the ever babbling machines you must daily

Give your life over to.

For the machine is the master of illusion.

*And the greatest illusion of all is that you
are nothing*

But a body of atoms or particles

Perpetually and blindly driven by ego,

Instinct, appetite and desire.

The machine serves this illusion

This maya of the body

And crushes all knowledge of the soul.

How necessary therefore it is to strive,

To awaken your self to the mystery

And the majesty of God.

In a sense-driven glitter of ephemera,

The work and worry of the world

And its ever more sophisticated machines

Drowns the soul's natural sense of this great
wonder:

The ineffable mystery of God and his Angels.

And if you do not withdraw regularly

From this tinsel glamour of the machine-
wrought world,

And go to where you can hear the one true
Voice

You will lose forever your natural sense of
wonder

And all contact with your soul.

For, in truth, your soul is an ethereal thing

A Holy Grail in which you find, and
nowhere else

Your true and divine Self.

It whispers to you across the ages of time:

Come, share in my great mystery.

The words you cull from the depths

Of your meditation therefore

Are like many multi-coloured butterflies

Which draw you away

From the evaporating mists of your measure of time

And into the sweetness of a truth far greater than any machine

Or mere body of withering flesh, can give.

For it is only in your meditation that you can transcend

The words that guide you here,

And in this transcendence you slowly learn

To replace the glimpses of your fading world

With the astonishing and enduring beauty

Of the vast and heavenly Countenance.

For these wingéd words are born out of a great mystery

Imprinted in the heart of the Earth

By the very feet of the Master of all masters.

They are the very food and drink of the soul,

The Cup given, to be shared by all

Who come to the Well

And there find waiting the Angel of Peace,

The beautiful wingéd Messenger of Love.

The Presence

Of all the arts that may be practised

None is more profitable than meditation.

For only when, in the depths of meditation,

You are emptied of the corrosive ways of
the world

Will you be able to feel the stir of Otherness

Which speaks of the mystery of your true Self.

The din of the world drowns out all knowledge

Of this deeper inner Self.

It can be nurtured only in silence, tranquillity
and serenity.

And if you do not know and nurture this
higher Self,

In truth all you do in the world,

All you say or feel will merely add

To the growing and terrible din.

For without this secret knowledge,

What is this world you live in

But a mechanical jungle of noise, a global
factory

That makes of humankind little more than
a mass-producing mob

Of screaming, empty, angry misfits

Drowning the pure sense

Of your sweet Otherness?

This sense of a real and ethereal Presence
in your soul

Comes to fruition in no other way

Than prayer and meditation.

Theologians and teachers may talk and write of it,

But this great truth of the divine Presence

Will never be more than a mere puff of pious wind

If you do not stir it substantially awake

By your sincere devotion to the Way

And its meditative disciplines.

For only then will you be able to distinguish the sublime truth

That is contained in these words.

Only then can you awaken in your soul

The wonderful and mysterious Presence.

Wait patiently therefore with your Cup by the still water's edge

Emptying yourself often of the world's din

And filling yourself

With the blesséd silence.

Your heart then will surely be lifted

And you will discern the true Voice of your soul.

This Voice may only whisper like a stranger at first.

But you become aware of its truth because it speaks to you

Of the Wisdom of the ages, a sublime knowledge

Which is inscribed upon the soul of every human being

But can be read only by those who actively seek.

Seek therefore for The Logos.

It speaks and speaks always

Out of a sublime knowledge of the eternal verities,

The virtues and truths that have survived

The ravages of time.

This Voice is not born of the passing world and its ephemera,

But is the very essence of the enduring and eternal Spirit,

The ever-present Spirit of God.

The Flame of Love

The Way of The Logos

Is the Way of love;

And love purified of all selfish desire

Is the only love worthy of those

Who seek to thread the Way of Wisdom.

This dictum is easy to understand but hard to live.

For, in a world where the sophistication of bodily satisfaction

Is the very dynamic of life, its business and its commerce,

And is the demand even of little children,

Whither the virtue of selflessness?

Who wants to hear of such things?

And of those who can hear, who dares to speak out?

But, in truth, it can be no other way in our world.

For out there the Voice of the true spirit

Is silenced amidst the all-consuming

Sense-driven glamour, glitter, and glare.

But know this, true seeker of the Way:

No amount of colour, costume or cosmetic

Can conceal the inevitable smell of death

That pervades all human flesh.

And only when in your meditation you have awoken

To the reality of your spirit,

Will you be able to fully open your soul

To this latter truth and its consequences.

But when you do, lo, how blissful the truth can be!

For then you learn that you will not die!

Yes. This body of flesh will certainly die.

But you have now come to know

That you are not your body only.

For the Angel being of your sweetest Love

Has guided you surely to a transcendent truth

That is not written in words

But is felt inwardly in the heart

Where you have patiently kindled the sacred Flame.

This Flame has nothing to do

With the fire of bodily or sensual desire.

For, compared with the uplifting, purified,

And sacrificial love of God,

Ordinary desire is nothing but a hungry
furnace –

The more you feed it, the hotter, more
demanding

And more all-consuming it becomes,

A veritable demon in the making!

The Flame of pure spiritual love however

Is chaste, sweet-scented

And lovely as a summer rose.

Meditate and you will find it.

The Flower Chalice

Raise up your face like a flower

To be kissed daily by the sun, that shining star

Which is more than just an ancient symbol of God

But a real intimation of God's truth, beauty, and love.

And yet the warmth we daily receive from it

Is but a shadow of God's great tenderness,

splendour, and majesty.

The flowers know this chaste spirit well.

Their very beauty reflects it abundantly.

And if you wish to know this true spirit of
Love

You too must bring the flower chalice of your
purest intentions

Often into the sanctuary of your heart

And place it there before the holy Flame

Of the great secret Spirit.

Pray then that your cup

Be filled with the balsam of virtue,

The lustral water that purifies the soul

And strengthens the heart of all humankind

Through the great God and his Gospel of Love.

You have begun your great ascent.

The Way of The Logos is raising you up

With the power of the purest dreams

Of prophets, poets, and patriarchs.

These dreams are whispered by your Angel

As often as you enter the magic circle

Of your silence and its wondrous peace.

Here you receive

The kiss of Life

In words that nourish not only your mind and heart

But are the very harbinger of eternity.

The New Birth

When you come to the Well of meditation,

Come expectantly, hopefully, and with earnest devotion.

Here you will be united

With the wondrous Friend of your heart.

See then how the desires, passions and lusts

Of your body of clay

Will slowly dissolve in the crucible of this higher union.

You will begin to feel the joy of a blessèd release.

You feel then the stirring of a new world

A new birth, a new body of spirit,

The spirit of the immortal Light of God.

This Light of the World can also be likened

To a heavenly bridegroom

Offered in a holy and sacrificial marriage to the Bride

Who is in truth your very own soul.

Therefore just as a man and a woman

Can enliven in their bodies the thought of love

And through this love a child is born,

So also does your own true and higher Self

Come to bodily life within the magic mingling

Of fire and water

Achieved only through the art and practise of meditation.

Know then, you who truly seek to enter

The Way of Truth and Wisdom,

That your heart must be tuned

To the hope of a new love and a new marriage,

A union which is holy, which cannot be undone or ever denied.

You have begun your journey back to God

Whose Presence is real, whose Being is eternal

Who promises rebirth

And whose only command is Love.

The Pastures of Delight

Numbed and every more numbed to the Spirit

Become the senses of human beings as they greedily climb

Higher and higher their false and seductive towers

Glittering like the paps of Babylon!

The glamorous chains of their supermarket world!

But to the heart that has opened

Like a star-flower to the chaste light of The
Logos

These towers of greed and ambition have no
attraction.

They are flimsy as a house of cards

And have no more endurance

Than dying flesh clinging to bones.

With courage, faith, and conviction therefore

Come often to this Well of Wisdom

And here give yourself up

To these fiery inspirations written into

The wondrous Gospel of Love.

The frozen world and all its evils then will
slowly melt away

And your Angel will appear

To guide your every step.

In tuning your heart to the divine
frequency of Love

You are shaping your soul, colouring it,

And feeding it with the very essence

Of immortality and Divinity.

Listen therefore to the Friend of your heart.

He says, 'My suffering and my sorrows are yours.

But be joyful!

For my triumph is also yours!

Awaken now to my Presence.

Sacrifice with me,

For your withering flesh and blood is nothing

Compared to the new risen body of ethereal Light

That I AM

And give to all followers of the Way of The Logos.'

Practise the virtues therefore

And sweetest of all sweetest joys

You will rise up from the death-dealing of
your world,

And like a splendorous and wingéd star-
flower

You will be wafted away from the dross and
the flesh-pots

Of your troubled genesis,

And the eyes of your soul will be opened

To a new world of spiritual Light.

Truly you will be reborn.

Make your way often therefore

To this Well of Wisdom

And drink deeply of its words

Of Love, Grace and Truth,

Words that give birth to new words,

Words that are the soul's purest nourishment,

For they point the Way to the stars,

And the heavenly pastures of delight.

BV - #0025 - 080321 - C0 - 203/127/3 - PB - 9780954025595 - Gloss Lamination